Come Dancing

A Collection of Contras, Circles, Squares & More

Daniel Clark

Copyright © 2014 by Daniel N. Clark
This printing, March, 2019

All rights reserved.

ISBN: 1495973158
ISBN-13:9781495973154

DEDICATION

For Barbara

CONTENTS

	Acknowledgments	i
1	Introduction	1
2	Circle Mixers	4
3	Easy Contras	11
4	More Contras	21
5	Squares	34
6	Circle Waltzes	39
7	Novelty Dances	43
8	Performance Dancing	47
9	Dance Classes	51
	Index	53
	About the Author	

ACKNOWLEDGMENTS

Thanks to Stanley and Relta Tucker for introducing my
family to old time community dancing, and for
hosting a wonderful series of community
dances at their home in
Milton-Freewater, Oregon.
Thanks also to Larry B. Smith
for passing on the fundamentals
of calling, to Penn Fix
and the Spokane Folklore Society
for broadening our dance horizons at the
Lady of the Lake Dance Camps, to Trudy Ostby,
Jon St. Hilaire, Carla Arnold, and all the other wonderful
musicians whose inspiring music always gets me out on the
dance floor—and to the dance communities
throughout the Pacific Northwest whose
hospitality and fellowship have
become one of my
life's greatest
joys.

1. INTRODUCTION

Come a Dancing

If you will come and dance with me,
A feathered cap I'll give to thee,
If you will come and dance with me,
Two red shoes I'll give to thee.
Come, my love, a dancing,
So far into the night.
Our feet will trip so lightly!
We'll forget that time's aflight.

-- French-Canadian song, 1775

Occasional square dances at the Prospect Point Grange near my home in Walla Walla, Washington were a fascinating part of our culture when I was growing up. In the 1970's, when I returned from California with a young family, we were invited to a monthly square dance put on by the Tucker family whose daughter Trudy played fiddle in the Ryegrass String Band. The dances were held in an outbuilding with a fine wooden floor on the Tucker farmstead in the Milton-Freewater, Oregon orchard country.

COME DANCING

In 1984, these dances started a transition from squares to contras, inspired by a visit that year to the Festival of American Fiddle Tunes at Port Townsend by caller Richard Bixby and several local musicians. Since 1985, when we formed our local folklore society, Walla Walla Friends of Acoustic Music, our dances have featured contras along with an opening circle, a waltz or two, and an occasional square, polka, or hambo.

When Richard moved away in 1987, we organized a callers workshop led by veteran Larry B. Smith. Since then, I've been one of the regular callers at our local dances, and have occasionally called at other venues around the Pacific Northwest.

Over the years, I've found myself composing many new dances, mostly contras. While some of these have been inspired by old square dance figures, and some I've seen danced in some fashion and have revised a bit due to faulty memory or with an idea about how they could flow better, most of them are simply mine.

In addition to calling and composing dances, my wife Barbara and I have offered a series of classes from time to time to help introduce contra dancing and other dance forms to our broader community, and to add enjoyment for experienced dancers.

I've also organized several performance dance troupes, including Bards of the Boards, an Irish ceili group; Shadrack's Delight, a contra performance group; and Frenchtown Dancers, a troupe presenting French-Canadian and Metis dances of the kind settlers in the Frenchtown area of the Walla Walla Valley were familiar with and were danced from Quebec throughout the fur-trading communities of western Canada and the United States by people of mixed indigenous, French, and Scottish descent.

Along with these activities, I've had the pleasure of organizing several contra dance weekends, as well as a variety of other community dance events.

This little book shares some of the benefits of those experiences, along with seventy-five of the dances I've composed.

Happy dancing!

2. CIRCLE MIXERS

A great way to get people dancing in a variety of settings is to begin with a circle dance, preferably a mixer.

The music used for most of the dances in this book is composed of 64 beats, usually divided into A and B parts, each of which is 16 beats long and is repeated once before going on. The number of beats for each move is noted in the call or description line.

Below is a simple dance for as many as will, with no partner required, though it's good to ask the dancers to distribute themselves somewhat evenly around the circle by their dance role as ladies or gents.

WASHINGTON PARK SHUFFLE

A1   All join hands and circle left—16
A2   Back to the right—16
B1   Into the center—8
       And then back out—8
B2   Ladies to the center & clap (on the 4th beat)—4
       Then back out—4
       Gents to the center and clap—4
       And then back out—4
Repeat.

After leading this dance a few times through, I normally drop hands with my corner while circling left, and lead the circle gradually into the center in a clockwise spiral before turning back counterclockwise at the last second to unwind the spiral, then turning again in a clockwise direction and picking up the hand of the last dancer once the spiral is unwound in order to re-form the circle and finish the dance with another iteration or two of the original moves.

PERSIAN CIRCLE

A1 All join hands and circle left—8
      Back to the right—8
A2 Into the center and back—8
      Ladies to the center and clap, and back—8
B1 Gents to the center and clap—4
      Turn left and swing your corner—12
B2 Promenade that corner—16
Repeat.

This variant of the traditional Circassian Circle couple dance was written during the Persian Gulf War. It's my favorite for beginners at community events, and is often danced just after the Washington Park Shuffle.

CLARK CIRCLE

A1 All join hands and circle left—8
      Back to the right—8
A2 Into the center and back—8
      Allemande right your partner—4
      Allemande left your corner—4
B1 Allemande right your partner—4
      Swing your corner—12
B2 Promenade your corner—16
Repeat.

This progressive couple dance has been very popular.

INLAND FOLK CIRCLE

- A1   All join hands, go forward and back—8
        Circle left—8
- A2   Circle right—8
        Swing your partner—8
- B1   Dosido your corner—8
        Allemande right your corner—4
        Allemande left your partner—4
- B2   Promenade your corner—16

Repeat.

This dance was written in honor of the longstanding Inland Folk program on Northwest Public Radio and its host Dan Maher.

JUNE CIRCLE

- A1   All join hands and circle left—8
        And right—8
- A2   Partners sashay counterclockwise—8
        (Gents in the middle)
        And back—8
- B1   Allemande right your partner—4
        Swing your corner—12
- B2   Promenade your corner—16

Repeat.

A vigorous dance. Note that the allemande in B1 is 3/4.

MISSION CIRCLE

- A1 All join hands and circle left—8
  Into the center and back—8
- A2 Circle right—8
  Go forward and back—8
- B1 Dosido your partner—8
  Swing your corner—8
- B2 Promenade your corner—16

Repeat.

Written for a summer dance on the grass at the Whitman Mission National Historic Site.

WALLA WALLA UNIVERSITY CIRCLE

- A1 All join hands and circle left—8
  And back—8
- A2 Into the center and back—8
  Balance the circle—4
  Rollaway your corner—4
- B1 Allemande left your new corner—4
  Swing your new partner—12
- B2 Promenade that partner—16

Repeat.

Written for a dance sponsored by our local Seventh Day Adventist college. After the balance in A2, gents roll their corner in front of them from their left hand to their right, while their corner faces them and does a half turn.

STRAWBERRY CIRCLE

A1 All join hands and circle left—8
      Back to the right—8
A2 Allemande left your corner—4
      Swing your partner—12
B1 Go forward and back—8
      Allemande left your corner—4
      Allemande right your partner—4
B2 Promenade your corner—16
Repeat.

It's strawberry season again!

SEPTEMBER CIRCLE

A1 All join hands, go forward and back—8
      Circle left—8
A2 Into the center and back—8
      Circle right—8
B1 Swing your partner—8
      Allemande left your corner—4
      Allemande right your partner—4
B2 Balance and swing your corner—16
Repeat.

Written in 1999 for the start of a new dance season.

NEW YEAR'S CIRCLE

A1   All join hands and circle left—8
       Back to the right—8
A2   Dosido your partner—8
       And swing your partner—8
B1   Long lines go forward and back--8
       Swing your corner—8
B2   Promenade your corner—16
Repeat.

For our 30th annual New Year's Eve Dance in 2016

TUMBLEWEED CIRCLE

A1   All join hands and circle left—8
       And back—8
A2   Dosido your partner—8
       Allemande right your corner—4
       Allemande left your partner—4
B1   Swing your corner—16
B2   Promenade your corner—16
Repeat.

Written for a contra dance at the Tumbleweed Music Festival in Richland, Washington.

COME DANCING

GRANGE CIRCLE

A1   All join hands, go forward and back—8
       Circle left—8
A2   Forward and back—8
       Swing your partner
B1   Dosido your partner
       Allemande right your corner
       Allemande left your partner
B2   Promenade your corner

For our old Ferndale Grange dance hall that is no more.

APRIL CIRCLE

A1   Circle left and right—16
A2   Swing your partner—8
       Forward and back—8
B1   Allemande left your corner—4
       Allemande right your partner—4
       Swing your corner—8
B2   Promenade—16

For a dance in April, 2018.

3. EASY CONTRAS

REBECCA'S CONTRA
Duple Improper

A1 Ladies allemande right—8
    Gents allemande right—8
A2 Dosido your neighbor, and swing—16
B1 Ladies chain across and back—16
B2 Circle left, actives swing—16
Repeat.

For my daughter Rebecca. Note that the allemandes in A1 are leisurely, using a full 8 beats.

WALLA WALLA CONTRA
Duple Improper

A1 Circle left and right—16
A2 Active couple dosido—8
    Actives swing—8
B1 Dosido your neighbor—8
    Swing your neighbor—8
B2 Ladies chain across and back—16
Repeat.

I learned a version of this dance from Sherry Nevins of Seattle at an event in Richland, so I called it the Richland Contra. Sherry began the dance with the active couple dosido in A2. Since beginning it with the circles in A1, it's now one of my favorites and I've given it a new name.

GRADUATION CONTRA
Duple Improper

A1 In long lines go forward and back—8
    Right hand star—8
A2 Dosido your neighbor—8
    Actives swing—8
B1 Down the hall in fours, actives in the middle—8
    And back—8
B2 Circle left—8
    Swing your neighbor—8
Repeat.

Written after a Walla Walla College commencement ceremony featuring several of our young dancers. This one originally ended in B2 with a ladies chain, but I've since changed it to add the neighbor swing—a crucial ingredient in any good dance!

CONTRA TO THE SUN
Duple Improper

A1 Circle left—8
    Dosido your neighbor—8
A2 Actives allemande left—4
    Swing your neighbor—12
B1 Forward and back in long lines—8
    Chain the ladies—8
B2 And back—8
    Actives swing—8
Repeat.

After many cloudy days, a salute to the return of the sun.

SHOWER CONTRA
Duple Improper

A1   Circle left—8
      Dosido your neighbor—8
A2   Forward & back in long lines—8
      Actives swing—8
B1   Allemande left your neighbor—4
      Actives allemande right—4
      Swing your neighbor—8
B2   Forward and back in long lines—8
      Circle left (same four)—8
On to the next and repeat.

Written one rainy summer day for a dance in Walla Walla's Pioneer Park bandstand.

LAKESTAR CONTRA
Duple Improper

A1   Left-hand star—8
      Allemande left your neighbor 1 ¾— 8
A2   Ladies allemande right 1 ½ — 8
      Swing your partner—8
B1   Circle left ¾--8
      Swing your neighbor—8
B2   Forward and back in long lines—8
      Right hand star—8
On to the next and repeat.

This is a variant of a dance I learned at one of the Lady of the Lake weekend camps sponsored by the Spokane Folklore Society, but couldn't quite remember.

REID REEL
Duple Improper

A1 Long lines go forward and back—8
    Circle left—8
A2 Gypsy your neighbor and swing—16
B1 Actives dosido and swing—16
B2 Circle left—8
    Actives allemande right 1 ½— 8

For an event at Whitman College's Reid Center Ballroom.

VALENTINE'S CONTRA
Duple Improper

A1 Gypsy your neighbor and swing—16
A2 Long lines go forward and back—8
    Circle left—8
B1 Chain the ladies across and back—16
B2 Right hand star—8
    Actives swing—8

For a romantic holiday.

A TALE OF TWO COUPLES
Duple Improper

A1 Gents dosido—8
    Allmde left your neighbor 1 ¾—8
A2 Ladies allmde right 1 ½ — 8
    Swing your partner—8
B1 Right and left through—8
    Ladies chain back—8
B2 Promenade neighbor across—8
    Swing your neighbor—8

For Charles Dickens!

CAMPAIGN CONTRA
Duple Improper

A1 Dosido your neighbor—8
    Right hand star—8
A2 Circle left and right—16
B1 Actives dosido and swing—16
B2 Down the hall in fours, actives in the middle—8
    Turn individually, return & bend the line—8

Written during a local political campaign.

POLKA DOT #2
Duple Improper

A1 Forward & back in long lines—8
    Ladies dosido—8
A2 Gents allmde right—4
    Swing neighbor—12
B1 Circle left and right—8
B2 Actives balance and swing—16

Written for an evening when everyone wore polka dots.

POLKA DOT #3
Duple Improper

A1 Forward and back in long lines—8
    Gents dosido—8
A2 Ladies dosido—8
    Swing your neighbor—8
B1 Down the hall in lines of four—8
    Turn individually and come back—8
B2 Actives balance, then swing through inactives—16

Another dance honoring the polka dot event..

OCTOBER CONTRA
Duple Improper

A1 Forward and back in long lines—8
    Dosido your neighbor—8
A2 Actives dosido and swing—16
B1 Down the hall in lines of four—8
    Turn individually and come on back—8
B2 Balance and swing neighbor—16

Written in October 2003.

RAINY DAY
Duple Improper

A1 Right hand star—8
    Dosido your neighbor—8
A2 Allmde right your neighbor—4
    Actives swing—12
B1 Down the hall in lines of four—8
    Turn individually, come on back—8
B2 Swing your neighbor—8
    Circle left—8

For a rainy April evening in 2005.

CIRCLE THE WAGONS
Duple Impoper

A1 Circle left and right—16
A2 Dosido your neighbor—8
    Actives swing—8
B1 Down the hall in lines of four—8
    Turn individually and back—8
B2 Right hand star—8
    Swing your neighbor—8

Remembering our pioneer forebearers.

JULY JIG
Duple Improper

A1 Forward and back in long lines—8
    Actives swing—8
A2 Circle left—8
    Allmde left your neighbor 1 ¾—8
B1 Ladies dosido—8
    Swing your neighbor—8
B2 Ladies chain—16

For a summertime dance on the grass.

PENITENTIARY PROMENADE
Duple Improper

A1   Forward and back in long lines—8
      Ladies dosido—8
A2   Gents allmde right 1 ½—8
      Swing your partner—8
B1   Promenade across—8
      Ladies chain—8
B2   Circle left—8
      Swing your neighbor—8

A pleasing escape from Walla Walla's prison.

NEW YEAR'S WALK
Duple Improper

A1   Circle left—8
      Dosido your neighbor—8
A2   Allmde right your neighbor—4
      Actives swing—12
B1   Down the hall in lines of four—8
      Turn individually and back—8
B2   Balance and swing your neighbor—16

For a 2006 New Year's Eve dance.

KENNEWICK KONTRA
Duple Improper

A1   Forward and back in long lines—8
Swing your neighbor—8
A2   Down the hall in lines of four—8
Turn individually and back—8
B1   Circle left—8
Actives swing—8
B2   Right hand star—8
Dosido your neighbor 1 ½—8

For a 2007 contra dance at the Kennewick Grange.

AUGUST CONTRA
Duple Improper

A1   Circle left—8
Forward and back in long lines—8
A2   Dosido your neighbor and swing—16
B1   Circle left—8
Left hand star—8
B2   Actives balance and swing—16

For a 2010 dance in Pioneer Park.

4. MORE CONTRAS

FOUR LEAF CLOVER
Duple Improper

A1 Circle left—8
 While still in a circle, 2's arch, 1's go under & turn away from partner, forming a four-leaf clover—4
 Balance four—4

A2 Circle left—8
 Open the clover, 1's pulling 2's through to ring the dishrag—4
 Balance four—4

B1 Swing your neighbor—8
 Ladies chain—8

B2 Swing your partner—8
 Circle right ¼, 1's arch, 2's under—8

From an old square dance figure, with very demanding timing in A1 and A2.

NEW LEASE ON LIFE
Duple Improper

A1 Dosido your neighbor—8
    Allmde left neighbor, gents allmd R ½—8
A2 Balance in a wave, R & L—4
    Allmde left your partner—4
    Balance again in a wave, R & L—4
    Gents allmde right ½—4
B1 Swing your neighbor—8
    Forward and back in long lines—8
B2 Circle left, star back—16

Celebrating recovery from a back injury.

BECKETT FOR BARBARA
Beckett Formation

A1 Circle left around the full set—8
    Circle right back to place—8
A2 Ladies dosido 1 ½—8
    Swing your neighbor—8
B1 Circle four ¾, swing your partner—16
B2 On the left diagonal, right and left through—8
    Right and left through across the set—8

For my wife and dance partner.

DIP FOR THE OYSTER
Duple Improper

A1 Circle left, actives swing—16
A2 Dosido your neighbor—8
 Circle left—8
B1 To the call "Dip for the Oyster,"
 while still in the circle, 2's arch, 1's go under
 and take a little peak, then back out—8
 To the call "Dive for the Clam,"
 while still in the circle, 1's arch, 2's go under,
 take a little peak, then back out—8
B2 To the call "Right on Thru & Open the Can,"
 1's go under, turn away from each other, and
 pull the 2's thru to ring the dishrag—8
 1's arch and send the 2's on to the next—8

Honoring another old square dance.

SPANISH SPRING
Duple Improper

A1 Gypsy your neighbor, and swing—16
A2 Gents allmde left 1 ½—8
 Gypsy your partner—8
B1 Swing your partner—8
 Forward and back in long lines—8
B2 Right and left through—8
 Ladies chain—8

For a 2009 spring dance.

WHIRLING DERVISH
Duple Improper

A1 Dosido your neighbor and swing—16
A2 Forward and back in long lines—8
    Actives dosido—8
B1 Ladies allmd left 1 ½—8
    Swing your partner—8
B2 Gents allmd left, pick up your partner,
    Butterfly whirl 1 ½ to the next couple—16

In B2, gents put their right arm around their partner's waist and back up and the ladies do the same while going forward for a butterfly whirl. Inspired by an interest in Sufism.

SPRING RELEASE
Duple Improper

A1 Gents allmde right 1 ½—8
    Ladies allmde right 1 ½—8
A2 Actives half figure eight above—8
    And swing below—8
B1 Actives up the center & turn as a couple—8
    Return with a half figure eight below—8
B2 Right and left through—8
    Swing your neighbor—8

In B2, the half figure eight begins with the follow stepping between the other couple and around the lady followed by the lead around the gent. In honor of the 2005 Spring Release of Walla Walla wines.

BARBARA'S THE CALLER TONIGHT
Duple Improper

A1 Dosido your neighbor 1 ¼ —8
    Balance in a wave, right and left—4
    Allmde right your N ½, G's allmde left ½—4
A2 Balance and swing your partner—16
B1 Forward and back in long lines—8
    Circle left—8
B2 Circle right ½, swing your neighbor—16

For my wife's calling debut in 2009 after I lost my voice.

FALL FANCY
Duple Improper

A1 Dosido your neighbor—8
    Allmde right N ¾, G's allmde left—8
A2 Balance in a wave, right and left—4
    Allmde right N ½, L's allmde left 1 ½—12
B1 Balance four right and left in a wave—4
    Swing your partner—12
B2 Ladies cross—4
    Swing your neighbor—12

For a dance in the autumn of 2010.

TUMBLEWEED CONTRA
Duple Improper

A1 Balance and swing your neighbor—16
A2 Ladies chain—8
    Right and left through—8
B1 Balance and swing your partner—16
B2 Circle left 1 ¼—8
    Pass through & partner push-off—8

Written for the Tumbleweed Music Festival in 2011. Note on the final four beats, after the right shoulder pass-through, a two-handed partner push-off in order to keep you moving!

EARLY MORNING
Duple Improper

A1 Gypsy and swing your neighbor—16
A2 Forward and back in long lines—8
    2's allmde right your partner 1 ½—8
B1 1's balance and swing, and face up—16
B2 Circle left ½ and pass through—8
    Dosido the next—8

Written at 3 a.m. on a fall morning in 2011.

THRU TRAFFIC
Duple Improper

A1 Ladies chain up and down the set—16
A2 Balance and swing your neighbor—16
B1 Ladies dosido 1 ½—8
    Swing your partner—8
B2 Circle left ¾—8
    Balance four and pass thru—8

Written as part of a composing workshop at the 2013 Lady of the Lake Fall Dance Camp.

NEW YEAR'S STRAIGHT SET
Quadruple Improper

A1 In two joined contra lines, circle 8 to the left—16
A2 Circle four to the left up and down the set—8
    Swing your neighbor—8
B1 Ladies chain across the set—8
    Swing your partner—8
B2 Circle left ¾ and pass through—8
    Dosido the next—8

This dance requires joining two improper contra lines across the hall, forming sets of eight up and down the hall. In A2, continue circling with the facing couple. If they like, couples out at the ends can dance with each other across the set, and for variety can cross over to return on the other side of the set. Inspired by a straight set Howard Ostby called at a Timberrib dance.

NEW YEAR'S GYPSY
Duple Improper

A1 Dosido your neighbor—8
    Allmde left partner ¾, gents allmde right—8
A2 Gypsy your neighbor and swing—16
B1 Ladies chain—16
B2 Actives balance and swing—16

For a New Year's Eve dance in 1994.

DAN'S BREAKDOWN
Duple Improper

A1 Balance your partner, clap right, clap left—8
    Dosido your partner—8
A2 Allmde left your neighbor—4
    Actives swing—12
B1 Circle left—8
    Swing your neighbor—8
B2 Ladies chain—16

In A1, after the balance, clap your own hands together on the 1st and 3rd beats and your partner's hand on the second and fourth beats. The percussion brings both energy and a smile!

FOLKLIFE CONTRA
Duple Improper

A1 Gypsy your neighbor and swing—16
A2 Forward and back in long lines—8
    Right and left through—8
B1 Ladies chain—8
    Circle left—8
B2 Swing your partner—8
    Circle right ¾ and pass thru—8

My takeoff on a dance called by Mary Devlin at the 1998 Northwest Folklife Festival in Seattle.

RASPBERRY JIG
Duple Improper

A1 Dosido your neighbor and swing—16
A2 Ladies chain—16
B1 Allmde right your partner 1 ¼ —8
    Forward & back, up & down the set—8
B2 1s half figure eight above—8
    1s swing below, 2s California twirl—8

For the California twirl, while facing the 1s, the 2's raise their joined hands, and the lady walks under the arch while they change places to face up. Written in 1999 when the raspberries were ripe.

WAVE THE OCEAN
Duple Improper

A1 Dosido your neighbor—8
 Circle left—8
A2 Couple #1 wave the ocean
 (1's arch over 2's, then back under 2's arch,
 and repeat)—16
B1 Circle left—8
 Swing your partner—8
B2 Couple #2 wave the ocean
 (2's arch over 1's, then back under 1's arch)—8
 2's arch over 1's again, and on to the next—8

Another old square dance figure. If it's a crowded hall, only the actives should swing in B1.

WALLOWA LAKE WEAVE
Duple Improper

A1 Dosido your neighbor—8
 Allmde right your neighbor 1 ¼ —8
A2 Ladies start a left shoulder hey—16
B1 Gypsy and swing your neighbor—16
B2 Forward and back—8
 Actives swing—8

For our Wallowa Lake Dance Retreat in 1996.

PROPER BREEDING
Duple Proper

A1 First gent, second lady forward and back—8
    Same two, dosido—8
A2 Second gent, first lady, forward and back—8
    Same two, dosido—8
B1 Allmde right your neighbor, 1st couple swing—16
B2 1st couple down the center, turn alone—8
    Return with a half figure eight around 2s—8

This is a proper dance beginning with leads on one side and follows on the other. In B1, the allemande is up and down the proper lines. Inspired by a session of English Country Dancing.

DOWNTOWN DOUBLOON
Duple Improper

A1 Dosido your neighbor—8
    Right hand star—8
A2 Circle left and right—16
B1 Actives dosido and swing—16
B2 Allmde right your partners all—4
    Swing your neighbor—12

For some dancing in a plaza in downtown Walla Walla at a summer performance of our Wednesday Night Band

FEBRUARY CONTRA
Duple Improper

A1 Forward and back—8
    Circle left—8
A2 Dosido your neighbor and swing—16
B1 Ladies cross, swing your partner—16
B2 Promenade 3/4 to end facing up and down—8
    1s half figure eight above, 2s cross over—8

Written for a winter dance at the Timberrib in 1999.

GYPSY CONTRA
Duple Improper

A1 Gypsy your neighbor, and swing—16
A2 Gents allmde left 1 ½—8
    Gents begin a left shoulder ½ hey—8
B1 Gypsy and swing your partner—16
B2 Forward and back—8
    Circle left 3/4 and pass through—8

This dance honors the spirit and energetic dancing of the Romani people, otherwise known as Gypsies. The gypsy in contra dancing is a face to face dosido danced "with attitude." The pass through in B2 is done with the right shoulder.

NORTHERN LIGHTS
Duple Improper

A1 Dosido your neighbor—8
     Gents allmde right 1 ½--8
A2 Allmde left your partner 1 ½, and
     Ladies cross by the right—8
     Swing your neighbor—8
B1 Ladies gypsy 1 ½, swing your partner—8
B2 Circle right 3/4—8
     2s arch, 1s under,
     clap right and clap left with the next—8

For the final moves in B2, dancers clap their own hands together, then clap right with the next, then their own again and left with the next. Inspired by this celestial phenomenon in the northwest.

CONTRA FOR CHASE
Duple Improper

A1 Dosido your neighbor 1 ¼ to a wave—8
     Balance right and left, slide right—8
A2 Balance left and right, slide left—8
     Swing your neighbor—8
B1 Circle left, actives swing below and face up—16
B2 Actives do a half figure eight above—8
     All dosido—8

After the dosido in A1, join hands in a wavy line across the set. After the balances, either slide or whirl past your neighbor and rejoin hands for a new balance, then slide again and swing. This was composed in honor of my visiting grandson.

5. SQUARES

MISSION SQUARE

A1 Head couples forward & back—8
    Forward again and dosido your opposite—8
A2 Allmde left your corner—4
    Swing your partner—12
B1 Four ladies grand chain—16
B2 All forward and back twice—16
    Repeat with sides
Break:
A1 Circle left and right—16
A2 Swing your corner—8
    Dosido your partner—8
B1 Allmde left your corner—4
    Grand right and left half way—12
B2 Dosido your partner—8
    Promenade home—8

For a summer dance at the Whitman Mission National Historic Site.

OCTOBER SQUARE

A1 Head couples forward & back—8
    Head gents swing your opposite—8
A2 Forward & back eight (in a circle)—8
    Promenade half way round—8
B1 Side couples forward & back—8
    Side gents swing your opposite—8
B2 Four ladies right hand star halfway—4
    Swing your partner—12
    Repeat with sides

Break:
A1 Circle left—8
    Dosido your corner—8
A2 Circle right—8
    Dosido your partner—8
B1 All forward and back twice—16
B2 Grand right and left halfway—8
    Promenade your partner home—8

If you want more variety, in B2 of the main figure you can have the ladies star ¾ and swing a new partner.

SPIRIT OF SPRING

A1 Dosido your corner—8
    Gents right hand star—8
A2 Allmde left your partner, allmde right your corner—8
    Swing your partner—8
B1 Head couples out to the right, circle 4—8
    Then back home and circle eight—8
B2 Allmde left your corner, promenade your partner home—16

Break:
A1 Forward and back—8
    Ladies grand chain—8
A2 Chain back—8
    Dosido your partner—8
B1 Balance and swing your corner—16
B2 Promenade your corner—16

Written in April of 2005.

AN EASY SQUARE
For Public Gatherings

- A1 Head couples forward and back—8
  Same four dosido your opposite—8
- A2 Side couples forward and back—8
  Same four dosido opposite—8
- B1 Allmde left your corner—4
  Swing your partner—12
- B2 Promenade your partner (or corner)—16

Break:
- A1 Circle left and right—16
- A2 Four ladies right hand star—8
  Back by the left—8
- B1 Four gents right hand star—8
  Back by the left—8
- B2 Forward and back, and repeat—16

For variety, the active dancers in A1 and A2 of the main figure can be either ladies or gents, and an allemande or an elbow swing can sometimes be substituted for the dosidos.

MARCUS WHITMAN
An Irish Set Dance

A1 Partners slide forward & back in closed position (step 1, 2—1, 2, 3), and repeat—16
A2 Circle left with a travelling step (1,2,3 1,2,3)—16
B1 Forward and back in a circle (using the 3-beat travelling or jig step), and repeat—16
B2 Dance at home (partners turn twice around with the 3-beat jig step in closed position)—16
A1 Ladies grand chain with the jig step—16
A2 Circle right and left with the jig step—16
B1 Big Christmas (form a basket & turn to left)—16
B2 Promenade your partner with the jig step—16

Note that the timing for the ladies grand chain is zesty, with four beats to cross the set and another four for the courtesy turn, and then eight beats back. The 3-beat jig or travelling step actually takes four beats—three equal steps and a pause—while the four beat slide step involves two slow steps and three quick ones. The Big Christmas is the basket figure where dancers put their arms behind their neighbors' backs and their right feet into the center, lean back to give weight, and use a buzz step to energetically turn the basket clockwise. Written for a 1994 St. Patrick's Day celebration at the Marcus Whitman Hotel featuring our Irish performance group Bards of the Boards.

6. CIRCLE WALTZES

WALLA WALLA COLLEGE WALTZ

A1 Circle left and right—8
A2 Forward & back, rollaway the corner lady—4
      Repeat—4
B1 Repeat twice more—8
B2 Waltz with the fourth person—8

The number of 3-beat waltz steps for each line is noted. For the rollaway, gents pass the lady in front of them from their left to their right hand with two waltz steps and the ladies facing the gents for the half turn. After the couple waltz in B2, gents leave the lady on their right. A long-time favorite.

SIMPLICITY

A1 Forward & back, rollaway the corner lady—4
      Repeat—4
A2 Circle left and right—8
B1 Waltz with your partner (or your corner)—8
B2 Promenade your partner (or your corner)—8

This is my favorite circle waltz.

WALTZING MALINDA

A1 Circle left and right—8
A2 Allmde right partner, allmde left corner—4
   Dosido your partner—4
B1 Promenade your partner—4
   Pivot back and return—4
B2 Waltz with your corner—8

For our musician and composer friend Malinda Pankl. In the second part of B1, while still holding your partner in promenade position simply turn toward each other and face the other way to reverse direction, each dancer keeping the same position on the inside or outside of the circle.

SANDRA'S WALTZ

A1 Forward & back, & roll away the corner lady—4
   Repeat—4
A2 Forward & back, roll away the corner lady—4
   Repeat—4
B1 Gypsy your partner and waltz—8
B2 Promenade your partner—4
   Circle back—4

For our friend and fellow dancer Sandra Cannon.

ANNIVERSARY WALTZ

A1 Promenade your partner—4
    Pivot back and return—4
A2 Dosido your partner—4
    Allmde right your partner ¾,
    Allmde left your corner—4
B1 Waltz with your partner—8
B2 Circle left—4
    Circle right and roll away your corner—4

Written for Barbara on our 33rd wedding anniversary in 2001. As an alternative B1, pass your partner by the right shoulder and waltz with the next, in which case the rollaway in B2 isn't needed.

NEW YEAR'S WALTZ

A1 Circle left—4
    Forward and back and roll away—4
A2 Circle right—4
    Forward and back and roll away—4
B1 Dosido your partner (or gypsy)—4
    Dosido your corner (or gypsy)—4
B2 Waltz with your partner (or corner)—8

For a New Year's Eve dance in 2002.

UPTOWN CIRCLE WALTZ

A1 Circle left—4
   Waltz with your partner—4
A2 Circle right—4
   Waltz with your corner—4
B1 Promenade your corner and pivot back—4
   Return, turn the lady under, and both face in—4
B2 Forward and back, gents roll away the corner—4
   Forward and back, gents roll away the next—4

For a spring dance retreat we organized in town, after several at a camp in the mountains.

UNITY WALTZ

A1 Forward and back, gents rollaway your corner—4
   Circle left—4
A2 Forward and back, gents rollaway your corner—4
   Circle right—4
B1 Dosido your partner (or gypsy)—4
   Waltz with your partner—4
B2 Waltz with your corner—4
   Promenade—4

Honoring the Black Soldiers Theater at the WWII Army Airbase, now our dance hall at the Walla Walla airport, where for some time the Unity Church of Walla Walla rented space to our folklore society for its dance series.

7. NOVELTY DANCES

THE WESTON MOUNTAIN ZIA
A Traffic Circle

The 1998 Weston Mountain Dance Retreat I put together for our local folklore society gave birth to a new dance formation.

While sitting around over lunch on Saturday, someone raised the question of whether it would be possible to have two intersecting contra lines. Though skepticism was high, a challenge is always healthy, so after the meal, I sat down at the registration table and wrote out what I called the Weston Mountain Traffic Circle, a dance with intersecting contra lines and an alternating square in the middle.

Following the afternoon workshop we tried it out, and it worked well and created a lot of excitement. When we danced it again on Sunday morning, someone pointed out that in Southwest Indian culture a figure with four sets of double lines coming out from a circle at ninety degree angles is called a Zia, while in modern times, it also resembles a traffic circle. Since that weekend, our Weston Mountain Zia and its progeny have been danced around the country.

COME DANCING

Here are instructions for our Weston Mountain dance:

Begin with four couples in a square formation. Ask the remaining dancers to form contra lines behind each couple in the square. The dancers then take hands four beginning at the square which is the "top" of the set, including the couples in the square. The dance begins with the four improper contra lines. At the end of the first time through, the four couples out at the top dance in the square, while the others dance in the contra lines. The square disappears at the end of the second time through and reappears in alternation throughout the dance. The dance is written so that a single call will cue both the alternating square and the contra lines. At the bottom of the lines, as an option to standing out, some couples may promenade counterclockwise around to the next arm of the Zia to proceed up that line. Multiple intersections can also be created.

Here's the dance:

A1 Circle left and right—16
A2 Allemande left your neighbor—4
Swing your partner—12
B1 Ladies chain (in the contra lines, chain up & down the set; in the square, do a grand chain)—8
Chain back—8
B2 Promenade halfway—8
Right hands (in the contra lines, star halfway; in the square, allemande your partner 1 ½)—8
On to the next (in the contra lines, pass through; in the square, turn and face the next contra line).

JUDGMENT DAY JIG
(Rapture Reel)
A Circle

A1 Circle left while turning counterclockwise on beats 3 & 4—8
Circle right while turning clockwise on beats 3 & 4—8
A2 Forward and back, and repeat—16
B1 Balance and swing your partner—16
B2 Into the center and promenade with someone new—16

This dance incorporates a bit of the confusion that was expected on May 21, 2011, the day the Rapture and Judgment were predicted by a well-known Christian Radio host, after which the world was to end five months later. Happily, we still get to dance!

SASHAY AWAY
A Flexible Dance

A1 Dosido your partner—8
Allmde right twice around —8
A2 Dosido your partner—8
Allmde left twice around —8
B1 Heel & toe twice, sashay out (G's left)—8
Heel & toe twice, sashay back (G's right)—8
B2 Balance and swing your partner—16

This couple dance can be done alone, or with one other couple, in a square, or in a circle for as many as will. After the swing at the end of the dance, face your nearest neighbor who becomes your new partner!

CLARK SWING
A Square

A1 Heads to the center with a right elbow—8
Sides the same—8
A2 Heads again with a left elbow—8
Sides the same—8
B1 Heads swing that special way (left hands in the air, Greek style, right hands around the waist)—16
B2 Now the sides—16
A1 Circle left and right—16
A2 Allmde left your corner—4
Allmde right your partner—4
Dosido your corner—8
B1 Swing your corner that special way—8
B2 Promenade your corner to gent's home place—16
Repeat with heads, then sides

Inspired by the exuberance of many folk dances.

POP GOES THE WIESEL
A Duple Improper Contra

A1 Dosido your neighbor and swing—16
A2 Actives dosido and swing—16
B1 Actives circle left with their neighbor lady—12
then pop her back to place under their arch—4
B2 Actives circle left with the neighbor gent—12
Pop him home under the actives' arch—4

The actives need to circle with each inactive 2 ½ times around in order to send the inactive through to their progressed position. In the spirit of the traditional song and dance of the same name.

8. PERFORMANCE DANCING

Bards of the Boards

The first time I saw Irish dance moves was at the Dacres Saloon in Walla Walla on St. Patrick's Day 1990 during a performance by our local Irish band Bards of the Moor. When the music got some of us up dancing, two women showed us the Sevens and Threes, a traditional Irish reel step. At Seattle's Northwest Folklife Festival on Memorial Day weekend, Barbara and I learned more moves, and by the next St. Paddy's Day we were back at the Dacres doing performance dancing with the band.

The following year two friends joined us to form a dance team we called the Bards of the Boards, We performed together for the first time at our Walla Walla Friends of Acoustic Music St. Patrick's Day show that year, then at the Cinco de Mayo fiesta in Milton-Freewater, at a folklore society coffee house in Kennewick, and for several other events. After that we gradually picked up more dancers and moves until in 1994 our twelve-member troupe was regularly performing and leading Irish ceili dances in the area.

Our repertoire included traditional Irish longways formations such as Waves of Tory, The Bridge of Athlone, Walls of Limerick, and the Haymaker's Jig, as well as some traditional set dances or Irish squares, along with some dances we composed ourselves in the traditional style. On a few occasions our troupe also danced and taught some Scottish country dances, though we weren't as comfortable with that more elegant style.

For about seven years our Bards group danced regularly throughout our region. People enjoyed watching us, and we had a wonderful time learning some of the more challenging performance dances such as the Fairy Reel and the High-Cauled Cap. We also enjoyed teaching others some of the easier figures and steps.

Though the ceili dances we were performing were not as demanding as the step dancing which has been made popular around the world by the River Dance troupe and its successors, my own knees eventually rebelled, after which we disbanded the group and replaced it in future years with a less-wearing but still enjoyable contra dance performance group.

Shadrack's Delight

Though contra dancing is for doing, not just watching, we've found that having a small performance group can be a fine way to enrich our community's cultural understanding as well to recruit new dancers. This is particularly true for a troupe that is able to integrate its performance numbers with plenty of opportunities for public participation.
After we laid down our Bards of the Boards Irish group, several of us formed Shadrack's Delight, named

after a well-known contra dance by Tony Parks. I've since learned that most contras can be performed by as few as two couples with very minor revisions to their final moves. The key is choosing dances that are interesting to watch, and then limiting the number of repetitions to approximately three.

As examples, the Four-Leaf Clover contra on p. 21 works as a performance dance, as does Tony Parks' Shadrack's Delight, Sashay Away on p. 45, the Marcus Whitman set dance on p. 38, Alternating Corners by Jim Kitch, and New Year's Gypsy on p. 28.

Frenchtown Dancers

A third performance group we've put together presents French-Canadian and Metis dances coming out of the fur trade era of the 1800's that combine Scottish and Irish music and dance traditions with French and indigenous culture. The mixed heritage Metis people of Canada and the northern U.S. have a lively and living square dance tradition that includes active jigs and reels, circle dances, and waltzes, among others.

Our Frenchtown troupe has appeared at a variety of local festivals to help publicize the Frenchtown Historic Site which I helped found in the Walla Walla Valley. We have used a simple jig step for most of our performances, which have included participation dances such as Drops of Brandy and La Bastringue, as well as some we've written or re-arranged ourselves.

Here's a performance waltz we put together and named for one of our members who was its principal composer:

GISELLE'S WALTZ
A Performance Circle

Begin with gents back to back facing partners

A1 With joined hands, each step to the right and left of the other, then gents turn the lady under your arched left arm on to the next gent—4
Repeat with a new lady—4

A2 Waltz with the 3rd lady, dancing out & back on the first two 3's, then once around on the next—4
Repeat, and end by twirling the lady to promenade position—4

B1 Promenade this partner for two 3's, then twirl the ladies in and form a circle—4
Go forward & back, then twirl your corner lady in for a ladies LH star—4

B2 Ladies turn the star & gypsy with the 3rd gent—8

Repeat 3 more times, ending side by side with a new partner in promenade direction

A1 Balance toward your partner and out, then roll the ladies from right to left—4

Balance toward your partner and out, gents arch and ladies go under to the next gent—4

A2 Repeat

B1 Weave the circle beginning with right shoulder—8

B2 Waltz with the 8th person, ending with a bow—8.

9. DANCE CLASSES

Contra dancing is a wonderfully vigorous, community-building activity. In 1992, in order to bring this healthy experience to more people, Barbara and I offered a beginning contra dance class at Walla Walla Community College, followed by a second advanced segment. The response to these weekly four-part sessions was good, and that fall we moved the classes to other venues, where they continued through 1996. Since then we've presented successful contra dance classes in a variety of settings over the years.

In our announcements for the classes we have often included the following quotes:

There is nothing so necessary to human beings as the dance...without the dance, a man would not be able to do anything....All the misfortunes of man, all the baleful reverses with which histories are filled, the blunders of politicians and the failures of great leaders, all of this is the result of not knowing how to dance.

--The Dancing Master in Moliere's <u>Le Bourgeois Gentilhomme</u> (1670)

Of course the merits of dancing are widely debated. A view contrary to the above praise was expressed by the Rev. J.D. Crane in <u>Popular Amusements</u> (1869):

The devotedly pious, the truly pure in heart, do not dance. Dancing wastes time, wastes health, scatters serious thought, compromises...character, leads to entangling associations with frivolous minds and careless hearts. Young people who are famed as "beautiful dancers" are generally good for nothing else.

In spite of that sage advice, we have persisted in our dancing pleasures, aided by the following wisdom regarding the flirtatious aspects of the dance from an unknown author:

A good dance should include respect and importance for partner, flirtatious possibilities, plenty of activity, and above all grace—a smooth flowing statement emphasizing the dancer's real life predicament—in short, an eight minute marriage.

In our classes, we try to accustom people to the fundamentals of hearing and stepping to the beat of the music and the musical phrase, as well as the basic moves of contra dancing.

Over our years of contra dance classes, we've introduced many people to the joy we experience together in our open, public dances. I hope this lively tradition will continue for many more!

Come dancing!

COME DANCING

INDEX

Circle Mixers
April Circle, 10
Clark Circle, 5
Inland Folk, 6
June Circle, 6
Mission Circle, 7
New Year's Circle, 9
Persian Circle, 5
September Circle, 8
Strawberry Circle, 8
Tumbleweed Circle, 9
Walla Walla College Circle, 7
Washington Park Shuffle, 4

Easy Contras
A Tale of Two Couples, 15
August Contra, 20
Campaign Contra, 15
Circle the Wagons, 18
Contra to the Sun, 12
Graduation Contra, 12
July Jig, 18
Kennewick Kontra, 20
Lakestar Contra, 13
New Year's Walk, 19
October Contra, 17
Penitentiary Promenade, 19
Polka Dot #2, 16
Polka Dot #3, 16
Rainy Day, 17
Rebecca's Contra, 11
Reid Reel, 14
Shower Contra, 13
The New World, 17
Valentine's Contra, 14
Walla Walla Contra, 11

More Contras
Barbara's the Caller Tonite, 25
Beckett for Barbara, 22
Dan's Breakdown, 28
Dip for the Oyster, 23
Early Morning, 26
Fall Fancy, 25

February Contra, 24
Folklife Contra, 29
Four Leaf Clover, 21
Gypsy Contra, 32
New Lease on Life, 22
New Year's Gypsy, 28
New Year's Straight Set, 27
Northern Lights, 33
Proper Breeding, 31
Raspberry Jig, 29
Spanish Spring, 23
Spring Release, 24
Thru Traffic, 27
Tumbleweed, 26
Wallowa Lake Weave, 30
Wave the Ocean, 30
Whirling Dervish, 24

Squares
An Easy Square, 37
Marcus Whitman, 38
Mission Square, 34
October Square, 35
Spirit of Spring, 36

Circle Waltzes
Anniversary Waltz, 41
New Year's Waltz, 41
Sandra's Waltz, 40
Simplicity, 39
Unity Waltz, 42
Uptown Circle Waltz, 42
Walla Walla College Waltz, 39
Waltzing Malinda, 40

Novelty Dances
Clark Swing, 46
Judgment Day Jig, 45
Pop Goes the Wiese, 46
Sashay Away, 45
Weston Mountain Zia, 43

Performance Dancing
Giselle's Waltz, 50

ABOUT THE AUTHOR

Daniel Clark has also written "A Privileged Life: Memoirs of an Activist," 2013, "Notes to the Self," 2014, "You are the Self," 2014, and has co-authored "Words: Dan & Barbara's Deathless Prose, and a Few Poems," 2014. He can be contacted by writing to PO Box 1222, Walla Walla, Washington, USA, 99362, or to clarkdn@charter.net.

032319

www.ingramcontent.com/pod-product-compliance
Lightning Source LLC
Chambersburg PA
CBHW071811170526
45167CB00003B/1272